# THE BUSINESS OF

# FASHION MODELING

*What you should know before entering the industry*

First Edition, Rev. 2

**Tondaleya Shamley**

Fashion Model Consultant

Dhymon House Publishing

P.O. Box 973253

El Paso, Texas 79997-3253

Telephone: 1-866-995-5588 Fax: 1-866-758-3709

Website: http://www.fashionmodelconsultant.com

Email: publicity@fashionmodelconsultant.com



ISBN: 978-0-557-67332-2

Cover art by Monica Tucker, Mocha Publishing.

Cover photography by John Hogan, Skydiverr Imaging and Veronica Chavira, Studio One Portraits.

All web links in this book are correct as of the publication date below but may have become inactive or otherwise modified since that time. If you notice a deactivated or changed link, please email publicity@fashionmodelconsultant.com with the words "Link Update" in the subject line. In your message, please specify the web link, the book title, and the page number on which the link appears.

The author does not guarantee results nor promote promises of results but rather present the opportunity for its readers to gain knowledge and understanding of the Fashion and Modeling industry. The content of this publication is not solely presented to guarantee results from the execution of recommendations and material presented. The author is not associated with any of the referenced websites or links. For questions or concerns with these references, please contact the company and webmasters directly.

Printed in the United States of America.

# Contents

# Contents

# Acknowledgements

This book is dedicated to my wonderful husband, Lindell, without his undying support none of this would be possible! You are my friend, my love, my hero, my life…thank you for always supporting me.

And, to all the aspiring models:

The decisions you make after reading this book will have a major impact on your career. So, make sure you remain proactive and continue to educate yourself. Take action on what you have learned and never give up on your dreams!

~Tondaleya Shamley

"Educate yourself; protect your dream by promoting yourself and becoming your biggest fan."

## Introduction

This book includes a comprehensive exploration of ***fashion*** modeling fundamentals, including terminology. These elements include the modeling business, self-evaluation, market-evaluation, research techniques, modeling career plan and execution of a modeling career plan.

An overview and insight to the various facets of the business world of Fashion Modeling, such as Runway, Commercial Print, Editorial, and Specialty Modeling are provided.

Upon completing this book you will understand and be able to demonstrate knowledge of:

- ✓ Self-Evaluation Techniques
- ✓ Market-Evaluation Techniques
- ✓ Researching Techniques
- ✓ Model Career Plan Development
- ✓ Model Career Plan Execution

# Chapter 1

## *Fashion Modeling Fundamentals*

Let's start with an overview of fashion modeling fundamentals and terminology. We will also identify the types of modeling categories and jobs that currently exist in the industry today.

### The First Steps

An aspiring model's first step is to learn as much as they can about Fashion Modeling.

Aspiring models should know what type of modeling they are interested in and what type of modeling best suits their personal aspiration.

They should know the type of jobs they are interested in pursuing and how to achieve them.

They should know what it takes to be a successful model and what it takes to become a professional model.

They should research and learn to adjust to the needs and interests of agents and agencies.

More importantly, they should know the responsibilities of a fashion model and approach their interest as a career or business.

The Modeling Categories

- High Fashion – normally ***runway***
- Glamour – normally ***commercial print***
- Petite – Sizes
- Plus - Sizes
- Teen - Ages
- Mature/Senior - Ages
- Body Parts – Hands, Feet, Legs
- Male – Boys and Men
- Character – To portray someone or something

The Modeling Jobs/Gigs

- Runway – walking on the catwalk
- Catalog – selling a ***product*** in a publication
- Showroom – boutique couture
- Fit – garment sizing
- Promotional – to promote a product or ***service***
- Television – acting in commercials
- Videos – professional or music videos
- Editorial – stock photography
- Print Advertisements – photographs for ***advertising***

Now that you know the diverse modeling opportunities within the industry, take a moment to think about what type of modeling you would like to pursue.

Remember to consider your physical appearance, ***personality*** and capabilities. For instance, a Fit Model must have perfect proportions for a given clothing size. Garment manufacturers and designers hire fit models as the standard sizing for their garments. Along with sizing, they are able to see how the garments move, and to help develop the garment patterns. A fit model's weight must never fluctuate.

To help with your assessment, answer the following questions:

What are the different types of modeling?

What type of modeling best suits your personality?

What is your most appealing physical feature?

Do you exercise regularly?

Do you meet the regular industry standards for height and weight?

Do you like performing in front of a larger audience or smaller audience?

Are you photogenic and do you like to be in front of the camera?

How easily can you take and follow direction?

Do you have sales experience?

How flexible is your schedule?

Are you interested in acting or performing?

## The Best Advice

There is no way to know if you have what it takes to be a model. The Modeling Industry is not focused on finding that one model to nurture into a Supermodel. The Industry is looking for models that can adjust and adapt to the demands of the industry. Additionally, they are looking for models that are able to sell their clients product's or services. This model could be one who has a particular height, weight, age, look or attitude.

The best advice that can be given when entering the modeling industry is to be very patient, persuasive and persistent. There are no easy routes to becoming successful in this business. It will take your hard-work and willingness to compromise, follow directions and accept rejection as a tool to improve.

A model's responsibility is to help portray an image that will sell a product or service. For a model, image is what generates the ability to get the job or not. Marketing companies use various forms of image to market a product or brand. It is the consumer's perception of the product or brand that generates product or brand interest and sales. Models used in a ***marketing*** campaign help to deliver product or brand interest to consumers.

In interviews with some of the most prominent modeling agencies in the country, they shared the following responses:

> *"Here at Nous Model Management in Los Angeles, we are looking for the typical model requirements plus a little something extra. There are always exceptions; however, the norm for most models is 5'8-5'11, dress size 0-6, and starting age between 14-21 years old. The "something extra" includes personality, professionalism and determination."* - Quoted from Mrs. Knight, Model Scout, Nous Model Management, Los Angeles, CA

> *"Client Preference. A client's preference is the motivating factor for the type and look of the model. Businesses often try to reach the masses of specific demographics. To do this, a full marketing campaign is created to include the type of model image they would like to project."The Young Agency uses size/measurements as well as personality to select models for their clients.* - Quoted from Mrs. Young, The Young Agency, Phoenix, Arizona

> *"The IT Factor! Personality, Beauty and Composure." The intangible assets that only an experienced agent could identify. Many agents see Beauty in many different ways. Selecting models are determined by who will be taking the photos, who will be marketing the advertisement, who will be preparing the hair and make-up. The collective efforts of these experts help to create the look that is desired.* - Quoted from Elite Model Management, New Faces Scout, New York, NY

## Chapter 2

---

### *Fashion Modeling Business*

This chapter will describe each component and provide a clear understanding of how the fashion modeling business works; as well as how you, the model, fits into that scenario.

There are several components that make up the fashion modeling business. Using a basic Marketing Model will help explain the core components of the fashion modeling business. These core components arc thc client, agency, model and consumer.

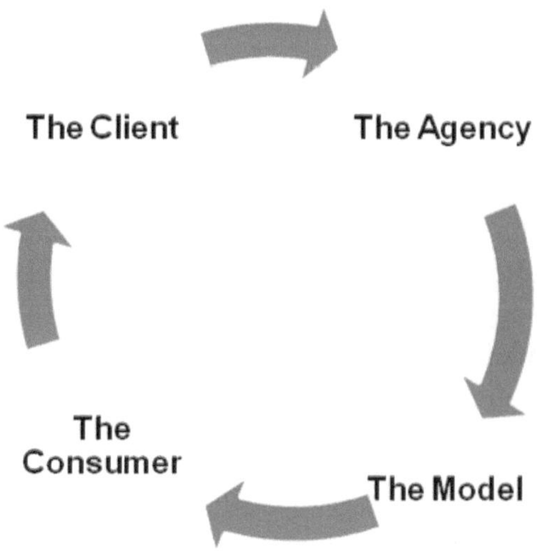


The Fashion Modeling Business Cycle

## The Client

The client is the person who generates the business idea that includes the use of models during a promotion or marketing campaign. The client could be a marketing agent from a major marketing company or an advertising agent from a major advertising company. Others may include production teams, photographers or producers. All of these business entities have a direct interest in selling a product or service. Their purpose for seeking assistance from an agency is to establish a target brand, market or ***demographics***. Models are often used to help reach these goals.

## The Agency

The agency is sought after by a client to help reach a particular target market. To do so, a client may ask that an agency provide a model that best reaches that market. For instance, a model that is athletic may be used to sell an energy drink. Commercials and advertisements are all about perception. If a consumer sees a young athletic woman drinking an energy drink, they perceive that the energy drink will have the same affect on them.

It is the agency's job to provide the model that best fits the requirements of the client. The client will use ethnicity, age and appearance to make a general assessment of their needs. Additionally, the agency will use personality and professionalism as criteria for modeling job referrals.

## The Model

As previously stated, the model is the end product to a marketing or advertising idea. The model is the one who will assist in selling a product or service. The way the model is presented is the way consumers will perceive the product or service. For instance, if a model is selected to appear in an advertising campaign for a teeth whitening toothpaste, then naturally, the model must have a perfect smile and relatable demeanor. The consumer must be able to make a connection with the model within 15 seconds of viewing the advertisement. Just one comment within the advertisement like, "wow, her teeth look great," can assist in selling the product to the consumer.

## The Consumer

The consumer is the person who will buy or use a business' product or service. The ability of a business to attract a consumer is a well-planned effort. Without the consumer, businesses are not able to thrive. Therefore, a business' ultimate ***goal*** is to reach out to consumers. This is often done with every creative and unique effort. However, in general, for print advertisements or even television commercials, models and actors are used just to project the purpose to buy a product or service.

In present years, consumers have become "shopper conscious." They are more understanding of the tactics used by businesses who wish to gain their loyalty. Consumers are aware of the large array of products and service that exist. They are aware of their choices. Therefore, it takes the efforts of the fashion modeling industry to help decipher those product or service characteristics that may be more appealing or beneficial to the consumer.

## The Client, The Agency, The Model, The Consumer

The collective efforts of just these major four entities of the fashion modeling business make up the core concept to the business. It is a cycle that flows from the client to the agent, then to the selection of the model who will capture the attention of the consumer.

Many believe that a model is selected first; however, explanation will show that in the business of fashion modeling, the client's needs are the major consideration and primary reason why a particular model is selected for a modeling job.

## Fashion Model Consultant

Consequently, I have often been asked how fashion model consulting fits into the Fashion Modeling Business scenario. I will briefly describe my services and how I assist aspiring models with reaching their modeling goals.

Fashion model consulting is a unique service. My consulting service is centered on meeting the needs of aspiring models. My services are often used before approaching or signing to major modeling agencies. I help to support and nurture the idea of becoming a fashion model.

As a Consultant, I assist aspiring models with preparing themselves to approach major agencies. In this business, the key is education and professionalism! With my assistance, you will be able to properly present yourself to major agencies throughout the world. You will also gain knowledge about the industry, agencies and what is expected from you.

This resource is a tool for reaching out to aspiring models all over the world. Many are hesitant about pursuing a modeling career because of the lack of knowledge or information. As a Fashion Model Consultant, I provide knowledge and personal consultation services to models who would otherwise attempt pursuing this career alone.

Therefore, to emphasize, I am **not** an agent or agency. I do not perform services that support client or model employment needs.

# Chapter 3

## *Self-Evaluation Techniques*

This chapter will help identify personal characteristics such as strengths, weaknesses, opportunities and threats. In the business world, this is otherwise known as SWOT. Using this method of self-evaluation will help to simplify the self-evaluation process.

Self-evaluation is the method of collecting and analyzing information for the purposes of implementing change or improvement.

There are several important techniques an aspiring model should incorporate when determining how he or she will benefit from a career in the modeling industry. The best approach in implementing your self-evaluation is to first answer various questions. The second is to perform three evaluation tests: Express, Test and Explore. You will discover that your responses help to establish a more sound decision in pursuing your desired modeling career.

### Evaluation Questions #1 – Interest

What are your personal modeling interests?

What do you enjoy doing?

What is your talent?

### Evaluation Questions #2 – Personality

To respond to the questions below, please select one of the provided responses.

How do you interact with others?

*I tend not to spend a lot of time with others.*

*I look for like interests and create dialogue.*

*I use more body language than anything else.*

How do you make decisions?

*I tend to flip a coin and use my luck.*

*I spend time analyzing the possible results to my decision.*

*I tend to seek the advice of others.*

Where do you direct your energy?

*To myself*

*To others*

*To the task at that given time*

How do others often perceive you?

*Outgoing and energetic*

*Professional and focused*

*Easy to get along with and kind*

Evaluation Questions #3 – Talent/Skill

What is your major talent/skill?

How can this talent/skill translate into modeling?

How would you categorize your talent/skill?

*Focuses on the Arts*

*Focuses on Business*

*Focuses on Human Relations*

*Focuses on Science*

Evaluation Questions #4 – Communication

Do you analyze information before speaking?

How well can you communicate without speaking?

*Not at all*

*Barely*

*Somewhat*

*Completely*

How do you find ways to understanding new information?

*By listening*

*By taking notes*

*By analyzing it*

*By asking questions*

Evaluation Questions #5 – Adaptation

How well do you adapt to new situations?

*I do not adapt well to new situations.*

*I tend to go with the flow.*

*It may take some time, but eventually I adapt.*

*I tend to adapt immediately.*

Do you often conform to or adjust the outcome of a situation?

To analyze the self-evaluation responses, collect only the responses to each question, listing them under each question topic. For instance, under the question topic "Adaptation" I will list my response "*I tend to adapt immediately.*"

You will now use these individual responses to identify how your responses relate to your individual SWOT model. Next to each of your evaluation question responses, identify whether that response is a:

S = Strength to your modeling career
W = Weakness to your modeling career
O= Opportunity to your modeling career
T = Threat to your modeling career

Assessment

Using your evaluation question responses, make a chart of your strengths, weaknesses, opportunities and threats.

Your listed "S" or Strengths are the main focus to help you develop your modeling career.

Your listed "W" or Weaknesses are those things you should focus on improving.

Your listed "O" or Opportunities are those things you will use to implement your short-term goals.

Your listed "T" or Threats are those things that you should try to eliminate or convert as an opportunity.

Now that you understand how the results of your evaluation questions will affect your chosen modeling career path, continue with the following testing method to evaluate how you should react to those results. The testing methods include:

- ✓ Express Yourself!
- ✓ Test Yourself!
- ✓ Explore Yourself!

## Express Yourself

From your previous evaluations, determine how you can express yourself. Figure out which characteristics best support your strengths. Remember this is all about how you communicate. It does not matter whether this is your strongest or weakest characteristic. You can learn from your interests, needs and values by looking at previous experiences, extracurricular activities, education and interests/hobbies.

This is especially important when learning how to project your own personal interests, experiences and personality upon others. Don't be afraid to be an individual. Show your creative capabilities.

## Test Yourself

One of the most appealing aspects of knowing and understanding your capabilities is to know yourself. To get assistance with understanding yourself, perform a Personality Test. The test will evaluate your interest, preferences and reaction to different situations. Based on this information, the test will allow you to develop a real good sense of the type of person you are and how your personality affects your decision-making.

Using the link below, perform a Personality Test through the Keirsey Temperament Sorter–II, Personality Instrument. Upon completing the list of short questions, retrieve the free "Mini-Report." Print the results for your reference. To access the website, open your internet browser and enter the following website address: **http://www.advisorteam.com/temperament_sorter/register.asp?partid=1.)**

Create and Explore Yourself

You can further explore your personal capabilities by becoming aware of those things that affect the way you respond to lifes' situations and circumstances. Take this time to complete another personality test that focuses more on situations currently affecting your life. Knowing how to control, react to or approach situations will be important to implementing and creating your modeling career.

Now, complete another test, which can be found by locating the Higher Awareness icon on the menu bar at www.fashionmodelconsultant.com. This short test will give you an overview of your current challenges, as well as guidance on how to overcome them. To access the website, open your internet browser and enter the following website address: **http://www.higherawareness.com?a_aid=d2878bd8.)**

# Chapter 4

## *MARKET EVALUATION TECHNIQUES*

This chapter will assist in identifying opportunities in your local market. It will also give insight as to how they will affect the level of success potentially obtained in that market.

Market Evaluation is the process of reviewing data sources about the performance of a particular market. These data sources contain information about demographics, potential and opportunity. There are several important techniques an aspiring model should incorporate when determining how he or she will benefit from a career in the modeling industry.

To begin the evaluation, first think about the modeling and/or fashion industry within your local region. Determine whether the local market is strong, average, weak or non-existent. A weak local market could possibly mean little opportunities. A non-existent market could lead to traveling or moving to a market that is more viable.

If your local market is strong or average, think about what major opportunities are available to models such as runway, commercial print or ***promotional*** jobs. Pertaining to the market, what types of models are comparatively used more for modeling jobs? Also, how do local businesses promote themselves?

There are three other important aspects to performing a complete market evaluation. A model should take into consideration the demographics of the consumers, the size of the population and the level of competition among local market models.

### Demographics of the Consumer

Determine the demographics of the consumer by identifying the age, income, education and ethnicity of those within your local region. This type of information identifies the target market of your local businesses. A business will use this information to improve their efforts of reaching the correct consumer. This also means selecting the appropriate model to attract that consumer.

Size of the Population

Population size is directly related to demographics. A model should know what portion of the population to which he or she will appeal. For instance, if a business is trying to reach college students, they know the general population, age, and income and education levels of those students. Therefore, a model that fits within the range of results may be used to promote products or services to those demographics or population.

Competition Level

A model will need to know how many, on average, modeling opportunities exist. Many times in smaller communities, there are very few opportunities; while in larger communities, there may be more. Nonetheless, being in one or the other does not guarantee any number of opportunities because the level of competition can be an altering factor.

This takes into account whether a local modeling industry is easier or more difficult to get in to, in comparison to the national or international industries. Consequently, a model should consider and understand the income potential for the local modeling industry and then determine its benefits, if they exist.

How you fit into the Local Modeling Industry

Overall, performing a market evaluation will help in determining how you fit into your local modeling industry. To make sure you understand how your local market affects your modeling opportunities, complete the following evaluation questions:

What type of modeling you wish to perform?

What is the location of your local region?

What types of local modeling opportunities exist?

What is the local demographic data to include average age, income, education level and the ethnicity statistics of the population?

## Chapter 5

---

### *RESEARCHING AGENTS/AGENCIES*

In this chapter, you will learn how to research, investigate and identify legitimate modeling agents and/or agencies. You will also determine which of these agents and/or agencies will be more beneficial to your modeling career.

Finding the right agent or agency can be perhaps the single most important tasks a model should complete. Without this step, a model could toss themselves into a whirlwind of disappointments and heartaches.

There are hundreds to thousands of agents and agencies throughout the United States. Knowing which ones are legitimate and most productive will narrow down your initial search. Well, there are ways of finding answers to those problematic issues and more. The next few sections will guide you through the process of researching agents and agencies.

<u>The Better Business Bureau</u>

The mission statement of the Better Business Bureau is *"Our Mission* is to promote and foster the highest ethical relationship between businesses and the public through voluntary self regulation, consumer and business education, and service excellence," (www.bbb.org).

Every state in the U.S. has local offices that support the efforts of the Better Business Bureau. This organization is used to report unfair business practices.

How does this benefit you as a model? A model is able to research to identify whether a business, such as an agency, has received complaints from consumers. Any interaction between a model and agency is considered a business transaction; therefore, if any such transactions falter against business ethics, a consumer can file a complaint against that business. Using this tool during your research can help you determine the business' worthiness of an agent or agency.

State Department of Licensing and Regulations

Every state has a Licensing and Regulations agency. It is a "regulatory agency that currently oversees over twenty types of businesses, industries, trades and occupations. The agency is responsible for issuing licenses, conducting inspections, investigating complaints, assessing penalties, setting rules and standards and holding hearings," (Texas Department of Licensing and Regulation).

Every business operating in any state must have a business license in order to conduct business in that state. This is required to help regulate the operations of businesses to secure the proper treatment of consumers.

How does this benefit you as a model? As a model and thus a consumer, you want to ensure that the business you work with is properly licensed and regulated for the benefit of the consumer. This research resource will also keep you informed of activities surrounding any one business or entity, such as the modeling and talent industry. By knowing the licensing business category of an agency, you are able to get information about its purpose and responsibilities to you, the model.

Hoovers

Many do not see Hoovers as a research source, however, Hoover's, Inc. is a business research company that has provided information on U.S. and foreign companies and industries.

Just by simply selecting a business category, you are able to retrieve information about the most productive agencies throughout the world. Each individual business report provides the name, address, phone number, email and website address as well as financials, key people and top competitor information.

This is invaluable to a model who is specifically seeking agencies that have a strong business base and productive service to its models or clients.

How does this benefit you as a model? Using information provided by Hoovers helps to eliminate a large degree of your overall research efforts. The company is highly known for its business research efforts and provides professional, detailed information.

Top 100 Modeling Agencies

Who are the top 100 modeling agencies in the world? By now, you could answer that question by utilizing the research methods provided in this chapter. But, there is also another reliable way to get this information without extensive research methods. Models.com is one of the most inclusive and well-presented modeling website portals today. It provides not only the opportunity to network and research information, but it also provides the latest in modeling and fashion news. One of the single most important continual tasks of a model is to stay informed and aware of the business of the modeling industry. The industry is ever-changing; so being informed could be the difference between getting the job and missing the boat.

The website provides a list of the top modeling agencies, top male and female models, forums, news feeds and answers to frequently asked questions. This is an awesome resource for aspiring models and those already in the industry. Be informed!

Model Networking Websites

Just like many industries, the modeling industry has means and opportunities for professional and aspiring models to network. The internet has made communicating with others of the same interest even more accessible and powerful.

Interacting within the online modeling circuit is a good way to get information about agencies, agents, photographers or producers; all of whom they have worked. There is nothing like getting a real-life account of the work ethics or reputation of any business. Networking can also provide models with opportunities that would have otherwise not been announced to the modeling public.

Photographers and Production Companies

Throughout this chapter, you have learned how to identify legitimate agents and agencies; however, it is also important to identify legitimate photographers and production companies as well.

Often, models are asked to perform modeling tasks for photographers and production companies. It is your right to research the photographers or Production Company's business and determine the benefit for working with these entities.

Always remember that a photographer or production company, in most cases, will not represent an agent or agency. They may have relationships with agents or agencies but they do not hold the responsibility of finding models for jobs or gigs. It is to your benefit to research a photographer or production company in the same manor as researching an agent or agency.

Using the research tools provided in this chapter, select one modeling agency in your city or state and complete a business analysis. To do this, you will need to:

- ✓ Select the agency.
- ✓ Research the Better Business Bureau for complaints against the agency.
- ✓ Research to see if the agency is licensed and regulated through your state.
- ✓ See if the Agency is listed under Hoovers.
- ✓ See if the Agency is listed by Models.com as one of the top 100 agency.

# Chapter 6

---

## *DEVELOPING A MODELING CAREER PLAN*

In this chapter, you will learn from a step-by-step guide on how to plan, develop and implement a viable modeling career. You will develop a modeling career plan based on your personal interest within the modeling industry.

<u>Modeling Goals</u>

A model should always set goals. The best way to set short-term and long-term goals is to use the SMART method (Goal-setting-guide.com). The SMART method is a way to evaluate your goals. SMART is specific, measurable, achievable and realistic goals that are measureable on a timeline.

**S**pecific: be very clear in identifying what goals you want to obtain, why you want to obtain those goals and how you plan to achieve them.

**M**easureable: establish a way to monitor your progress.

**A**chievable: establish goals that are obtainable and think about those opportunities that can bring you closer to your goals.

**R**ealistic: always set realistic goals and know that it is one that is obtainable.

**T**imeline: use time to measure your achievements and set clear target timeframes.

Requirements

What are the requirements of a model?

Mentally:

> Are you able to take criticism?
> Are you creative and knowledgeable about fashion?
> Are you focused and able to follow direction?
> Are you able to work as a team?

Physically:

> What is your age?
> What is your height?
> What is your weight?
> What are your measurements?
> Do you have unique facial features and skin?

Skills and Interest

The best way for a model to introduce their skills and interest is to develop a modeling resume that includes an introduction, list of experience or talents and a description of your interest.

In creating your modeling resume, you would have identified those skills and interest that could enhance your modeling career.

- ✓ Identify your personal attributes which complement the physical and mental requirements of a model.
- ✓ Create your modeling resume' and target agent/agency list.
- ✓ Establish a target date to develop modeling photographs.

There are several skills used predominately by models: fashion and beauty knowledge, personality, self-discipline, positive attitude, professionalism, creativity and being photogenic. Although there are no educational requirements to become a model, it is always helpful to have obtained skills in the arts, drama, and dance or fashion design.

Materials/Resource

A model will identify those materials or resources that are needed while pursuing a modeling career. Typical materials include photographs or portfolio, model resume and a target list of agents/agencies.

Analysis

The process of analysis is to perform a thorough examination of the parts that make up a whole. At this point, you should review the content of this chapter and determine the main focus of your modeling career plan. *List your modeling goals using the SMART method.*

The Plan

The plan is your proposed intent to complete tasks with the purpose of achieving a goal. Now that you have analyzed your modeling career plan, it is time to put it all into action. Assign a timeline to the achievement of your modeling career plan goals. Remember, your goals should use the SMART method and be made very clear and concise. You will implement this plan during the next chapter, "Executing your Modeling Career Plan."

# Chapter 7

## *EXECUTING YOUR MODELING CAREER PLAN*

In this chapter, you will learn from a step-by-step guide on how to execute your modeling career plan to include producing and developing photographs, marketing yourself to industry businesses, maintaining your career and self-improvement.

### Marketing Yourself - Photographs

Your first tool of business is your photographs. It does not matter whether they are snap shots, professional shots, a portfolio or a collaboration of photographs; but you must have some form of photographs prepared to present to agents or agencies.

To further elaborate on photograph preparation, once you have researched the agencies you wish to pursue you will need to provide photographs in the required format. This information is provided on the agency's website, you will need to locate the section that gives guidance to aspiring new models.

Of course preparing photographs specifically for each agency you wish to contact can become expensive. Therefore, I recommend that you prepare "Photo Cards." Photo cards are a photo technique I created to meet the demanding needs of the agencies. Do not get this confused with Composite (Comp) Cards or ***SED Cards***.

A photo card includes four to six photographs on a 5x8 size photo paper. The front of the card includes profile head shots without make-up and one large photograph with make-up including your name. The back of the card includes at least 2 photographs that are full-body shots and three-quarter shots. The photographs on the photo card should be very natural, crisp and clear. They should show your range of personality and versatility.

Create a list of at least three fashion photographers in your local area. Research these photographers to determine if they are able to create the photographs you will need for your photo card.

You should schedule appointments with the photographers to review their work before hiring them to do your photo shoots.

## Marketing Yourself - Online

Our previous form of marketing yourself with photographs requires physically mailing your photos to a potential agent or agency. With the use of the internet, you could eliminate the use of "snail mail," cost of duplicating the photos and purchasing stamps.

In the case of using the internet to market yourself, you could create a model website. This website could be used to display your photographs, provide background information such as your model resume and provide contact information.

When using this form of markcting, you will be required to use heavy advertising to get potential agents or agencies to your website. Also, you will need to be very careful with the type of information you provide. Remember, the internet is viewed by everyone and not one specific person.

Another and cost effective way to market you online are to join a modeling portfolio hosting website. These website normally charge a monthly fee. They also provide the opportunity to directly reach agents or agencies. Some of these types of hosting websites provide modeling information, news and networking opportunities.

The downsides to these portfolios hosting websites are that some host hundreds and thousands of model photographs. With so many, your personal portfolio could get lost in the masses.

Research these hosting websites to find out which would be most beneficial to you. Determine how successful the opportunity has been for other models.

## Self-Improvement

This information has helped you move towards the direction of self-improvement. Maintaining self-improvement can be challenging but is a necessity in this business. Listed below are a few ways to help maintain your self-improvement:

**Stay positive**. Thinking positive helps you to focus on your opportunities.

**You are the attraction**. Pull people towards you by displaying your desires.

**Be persistent.** Take action daily-there is no easy way to pursuing this career.

**Get Support.** Have a support group or partner to help you stay focused and be encouraged.

**Portions of this information provided by JD Marshall, Confident Lifestyle*

Maintaining Your Career

Pursuing a modeling is a career and requires much effort. At this point, your efforts should be maintained. It can often be very difficult; however, your focus should be on your appearance, skills, knowledge and business strategy. These are things that will change and should, continuously.

- ✓ Always seek ways to improve your appearance.
- ✓ Improve on your skills through training.
- ✓ Seek knowledge and information about the industry.
- ✓ Revisit your business strategy regularly and adjust as needed.

## Conclusion

You have now completed all seven chapters of this book including completing the tasks assigned. You are now ready to enter the modeling industry more professionally prepared and equipped with the tools to get your foot in the door.

Take the time to reflect on the information you have learned from this book, along with your completed research and assignments. Your well thought-out plan will be your first step to a successful modeling career.

Remember, your individual results and successes may vary, and all provided information is not intended to guarantee results but to supply information to assist with your professional development. Your passion, will and hard work will determine where you go in your interest within the fashion modeling industry.

## Glossary

It will be important that you review these terms and become familiar with their usage and meaning.

***Advertising*** - Making known; calling public attention to a product, service, or company by means of paid announcements so as to affect perception or arouse consumer desire to make a purchase or take a particular action. (Motto)

***Branding*** - The process of creating a brand, the visual, emotional, rational, and cultural image associated with a company or a product. (Kathman, 2005)

***Casting Call*** - A notice put out by a producer, art director or casting director of an opportunity in a film, video, commercial or print project. (ModelingSeminars.com)

***Collection/Line*** – A group of exclusive clothing designed by a designer.

***Commercial Print*** – A collection of photographs normally used for print publications such as catalogs or magazines.

***Comp Card*** – Composite card is the formal name. It is a card with several photos of a model that also includes their statistics and contact information. This is submitted to agents/agencies for consideration and normally serves as a portfolio and business card.

## Glossary

***Demographics*** - The description of a group of consumers, most often age, gender, household income, level of education, marital status, employment status, number of people in the household, and region of the country. (Theidm)

***Exclusive*** - The rights granted to an entity, under contract, are given to only that entity, not shared with others.

***Fashion*** - Consumer goods (especially clothing) in the current mode. (Princeton)

***Gig*** - A slang term for a job or a booking. (Aeispeakers)

***Goal*** - the result or achievement toward which effort is directed; aim; end. (dictionary.com)

***Haute Couture*** - Trend-setting fashions (Princeton)

***High Fashion*** - Same as haute couture; the most exclusive designs, often unique pieces created for individual customers. (Glencoe)

***Marketing*** - The way a business organization identifies its customers, defines and develops the products or services that its customers want, and sells and distributes those products or services to customers.

***Non-Exclusive*** - The rights granted to an entity, under contract, are not given just to one entity.

***Open Call*** – An interview or audition often conducted by agents/agencies to allow aspiring models to be considered without an appointment or invitation.

## Glossary

***Personality*** - The complex of all the attributes--behavioral, temperamental, emotional and mental--that characterize a unique individual. (Princeton.edu)

***Photo Shoot*** - Generally used in the fashion industry, whereby a Model poses for a photographer at a studio where multiple photos are taken for a particular modeling job. (Wikipedia)

***Product*** – In marketing, a product is anything that can be offered to a market that might satisfy a want or need. (Kotler, et al., 2006)

***Promotional*** - A promotional model is a person hired to drive consumer demand or increase awareness for a product, service, brand, or concept by directly interacting with consumers or usually through their appearance or acting. (Wikipedia)

***Runway/Catwalk*** - A term probably derived from catwalks that connect adjacent buildings describes a narrow, usually elevated platform used by models to demonstrate clothing and accessories during a fashion show. (Wikipedia)

***SED Card*** – Similar to a Comp Card, a term often used in Europe to describe a model's compilation of photographs that is created into a card and submitted to agents/agencies to be considered for modeling jobs.

***Service*** - In economics and marketing, a service is the non-material equivalent of a good. (Wikipedia)

## References


JD Marshall, Confident Lifestyle, retrieved 4/20/2009, posted at www.confident-lifestyle.com.

Keirsey Temperament Sorter–II, Personality Instrument. Mini-Report retrieved 5/01/2009, posted at website Keirsey, http://www.advisorteam.com/temperament_sorter/register.asp?partid=1

Higher Awareness, retrieved 2/15/2009, posted at website http://www.higherawareness.com?a_aid=d2878bd8

Texas Department of Licensing and Regulation, retrieved 5/6/2009 posted at website http://www.license.state.tx.us/

Goal Setting Guide, 2009, posted at website, www.Goal-setting-guide.com.

Better Business Bureau, retrieved 3/1/2009, posted at website, http://www.bbb.org

Michael J. Motto, retrieved 2/1/2009, posted at website, http://www.motto.com/glossary.html

Theidm, retrieved 1/18/2009, posted at website, www.theidm.com

Princeton, retrieved 2/20/2009, posted at website, www.princeton.edu

Model Seminars of America, retrieved 6/9/2009 posted at website, http://www.modelingseminars.com/definitions.html

## References

Kathman, Jerry (2005) Building Leadership Brands by Design, All Business - Branding, retrieved 5/24/09, posted at website http://www.allbusiness.com/marketing-advertising/strategic-marketing/906652-1.html

AEI Speakers Bureau, retrieved 4/28/2009, posted at website, http://www.aeispeakers.com/definitions.php

Dictionary.com, retrieved 8/1/2009, posted at website, http://dictionary.reference.com/browse/goal

Marketing Essentials, DECA Connections, retrieved 7/13/2009, posted at website, http://www.glencoe.com/sec/busadmin/marketing/dp/ap_and_acc_mktg/gloss.shtml

Wikipedia, The Free Encyclopedia, several references retrieved 3/2/2009, posted at website, www.wikipedia.org

Kotler, et all (2006) The Principles of Marketing, retrieved from Wikipedia, The Free Encyclopedia 8/28/2009

## About the Author

Tondaleya D. Shamley was born and raised in Prince Georges County, Maryland. She is a Fashion Model Consultant that has spent over 30 years in the fashion and modeling industry; owning and operating modeling agencies in the Washington, D.C. area and Germany.

Mrs. Shamley has earned a Bachelors of Science Degree in Fashion Merchandising and Textiles from the University of Maryland Eastern Shore, Masters of Business Administration from the University of Phoenix, and successful completion of the Alternative Teaching Certification Program at the University of Texas at El Paso. She has developed skills which are vital to the fashion and modeling industries.

Mrs. Shamley has taken pride in developing a business that not only educates but also inspires individuals to pursue their dreams. *"I enjoy consulting, teaching and writing. I use simple formats and pertinent topics. I use life experiences and life knowledge of expression to create my topics, titles and articles. I am an amateur writer who uses writing to stimulate thought, conversation, debate or a need to know. I do not acknowledge to know everything, I acknowledge to want to increase my knowledge through good ole' fashion research and expert conversation."*

Mrs. Shamley has dedicated numerous volunteer hours to her communities and a plethora of projects. As Editor-in-Chief of epStyle e-Magazine, she has nurtured the successful inclusion of a unique style publication. She is the Fashion/Style Key Contributor for Army Wife Magazine, Fort Bliss Life, and the El Paso Fashion Examiner and numerous blogs. She takes pride in sharing her talent and knowledge about the modeling and fashion industries and has developed a very unique learning concept for local models. She is the Creator and Competition Coordinator of the El Paso Ultra Model Competition. She serves as Fashion

Model Consultant to aspiring models; offering online chat capabilities to aspiring models who need individual assistance and host an online talk radio show, YFMC Radio, offering weekly shows about the fashion and modeling industry to include special guests. She is a University of Texas at El Paso Community Enrichment Program instructor for a class entitled "So You want to be a Fashion Model". She serves as Director of the Coalition of Fashion Professionals, El Paso which supports her views of preserving ethical business practices within the fashion and modeling industries.

This book is just the beginning for Mrs. Shamley, as she journeys and learns from the ever-changing industry of fashion modeling. She has been married to her Army retired husband for 10 years and has two sons, TreVion and Troey. Her industry motto is "Educate yourself; protect your dream by promoting yourself and becoming your biggest fan."

> *"I am the product of two very intelligent and hardworking people. Making a mark in my own world has come with a price. Dedication and perseverance are my secret to success. Not only have I equipped myself with knowledge and education but also with confidence and self-esteem, often needed to beat the odds of the world. I was never painted a pretty picture nor had all my needs placed in my hand. I am the product of what can only be described as a woman who knows she can."*

**Contact the Author:**

DHP
Dhymon House Publishing
P.O. Box 973253, El Paso, Texas.
Phone: 1-866-995-5588.
Email: tondaleya@fashionmodelconsultant.com

To continue to receive support and assistance with your modeling career, visit www.fashionmodelconsultant.com to ChatLive and tune into weekly discussions on Your Fashion Model Consultant Talk Radio (YFMC Radio) at http://www.blogtalkradio.com/yfmc. You can also continue following Mrs. Shamley on Twitter, www.twitter.com/tshamley and Facebook, www.facebook.com/fashionmodelconsultant.

www.ingramcontent.com/pod-product-compliance
Ingram Content Group UK Ltd.
Pitfield, Milton Keynes, MK11 3LW, UK
UKHW041833200726
13854UKWH00003BA/1120

9 780557 673322